GEOLOGY ROCKS!

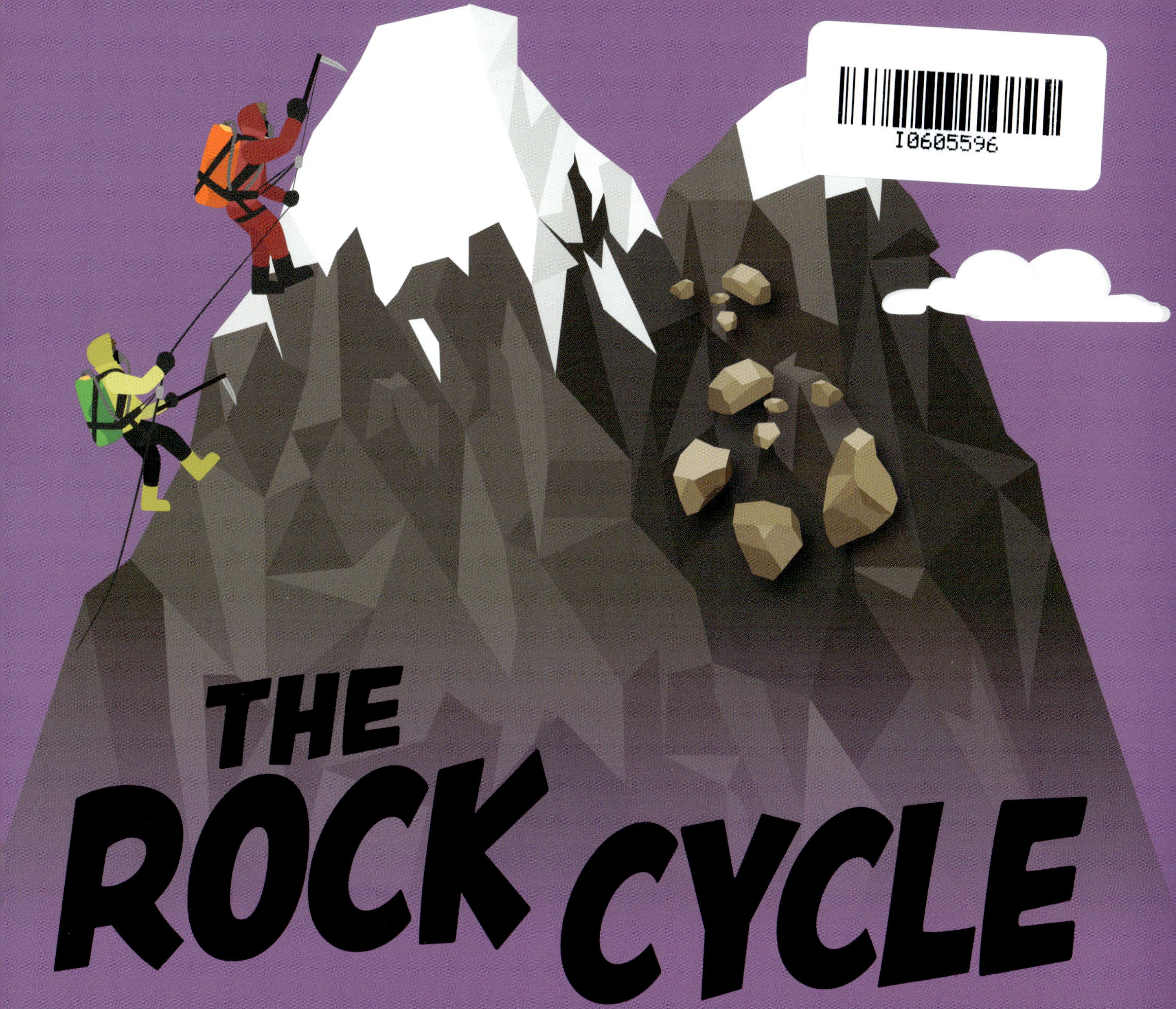

THE ROCK CYCLE

CLAUDIA MARTIN

Please visit our website, www.garethstevens.com. For a free color catalog of all our high-quality books, call toll free 1-800-542-2595 or fax 1-877-542-2596.

Published in 2025 by
Gareth Stevens Publishing
2544 Clinton St.
Buffalo, NY 14224

First published in Great Britain in 2023 by Wayland

Author and editor:
Claudia Martin

Designer:
Clare Nicholas

Series designer:
Rocket Design (East Anglia) Ltd

Illustrator:
Steve Evans

Proofreader:
Annabel Savery

BE CAREFUL!

- Wear an apron and cover surfaces.
- Tie back long hair.
- Ask an adult for help with cutting.
- Check materials for allergens.

We recommend adult supervision at all times while doing the activities in this book. Always be aware that materials may contain allergens, so check the packaging for allergens if there is a risk of an allergic reaction. Anyone with a known allergy must avoid these.

Cataloging-in-Publication Data
Names: Martin, Claudia.
Title: The rock cycle / Claudia Martin.
Description: Buffalo, NY : Gareth Stevens Publishing, 2025. | Series: Geology rocks! | Includes glossary and index.
Identifiers: ISBN 9781538293935 (pbk.) | ISBN 9781538293942 (library bound) | ISBN 9781538293959 (ebook)
Subjects: LCSH: Rocks--Juvenile literature. | Geochemical cycles--Juvenile literature.
Classification: LCC QE432.2 M37 2025 | DDC 552--dc23

Picture acknowledgements: Shutterstock: Andrii_M front cover tc, 1tc, parose front cover tl, 1tl, greenpic.studio back cover l, 9tr, 13bl, 25cr, Amadeu Blasco back cover cl, 14bl, 16bc, stihii back cover c, 15br, 24b, Merkushev Vasiliy back cover r, 8–9b, Virinaflora 2tr, Alexlukin 3tr, 21bl, christographerowens 3cr, 13tr, Bjoern Wylezich 3br, 4br, Gigi Peis 3bl, 23b, TuktaBaby 4bl, Tyler Boyes 4bc, VectorMine 5c, 10bc, 20b, 22bc, Colin Hayes 6cl, 30tl, Designua 7cl, Elena Arkadova 9cr, Slatan 11tr, tenkl 11b, Helen Hotson 12b, Claudia G Cooper 13cl, Emir Kaan 14br, Raphael Rivest 15tl, zombiu26 15bl, Budilnikov Yuriy 17bl, BlueRingMedia 18bc, Dirk M. de Boer 19tr, Aleksandr Pobedimskiy 21tl, 21cr, Yes058 Montree Nanta 21tr, 21cl, 23cr, Sakdinon Kadchiangsaen 21br, mahirart 23cl, EreborMountain 25t, Sihasakprachum 25b, Zamytskiy Leonid 26cr, goran_safarek 26bl, SAPHotog 27tr, Nigel Jarvis 27cl, Hayk_Shalunts 27br, Ralf Lehmann 28t, Bibadash 31t, ProStockStudio 31cr, klyaksun 32b; Steve Evans: 7br, 11tl, 15tr, 17br, 21br, 23bl, 27bc, 29b.

All additional design elements from Shutterstock or drawn by designer.

Printed in the United States of America

CPSIA compliance information: Batch #CSGS25: For further information contact Gareth Stevens at 1-800-542-2595.

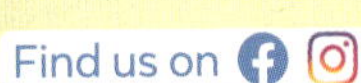

CONTENTS

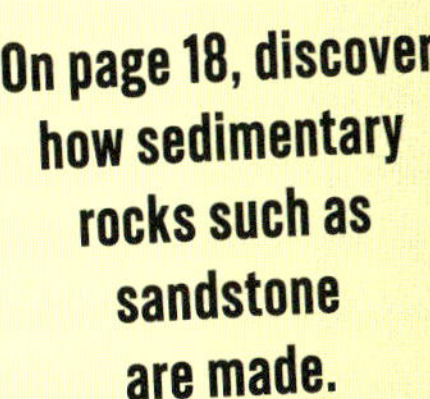

On page 18, discover how sedimentary rocks such as sandstone are made.

What made the cracks in this limestone? Find out on page 13.

Find out which minerals make up lapis lazuli on page 4.

WHAT IS THE ROCK CYCLE?

Rock is always changing—very, very slowly.

Wherever you are, there is rock beneath your feet, even if it is hidden by buildings or grass. Rock seems unchanging, but it is constantly being made and destroyed. The rock cycle is all the processes that change Earth's rock.

Rock groups

Rocks are mixtures of minerals. Minerals are solids that form in the ground or water. For example, the rock lapis lazuli is a mixture of the blue mineral lazurite, white mineral calcite, and gold mineral pyrite. There are three groups of rocks, each of them made in a different way:

IGNEOUS

Basalt is an igneous rock.

Igneous rocks are made when melted rock—called magma—cools into solid rock, either beneath Earth's surface or when hot rock erupts from a volcano. See page 22.

SEDIMENTARY

Chalk is a sedimentary rock.

Sedimentary rocks are made when bits of rock, mineral, or dead animals and plants, called sediment, become stuck together. See page 18.

METAMORPHIC

I'm soooo pretty.

Lapis lazuli is a metamorphic rock.

Metamorphic rocks are made when any rock is heated or pressed beneath Earth's surface. See page 20.

Change, change, change ...

The rock cycle changes rocks from one group into another group, over and over again.

QUICK QUIZ!

How old is Earth's youngest rock:
1 billion years old,
1 million years old,
or less than 1 year old?

Answer on page 28.

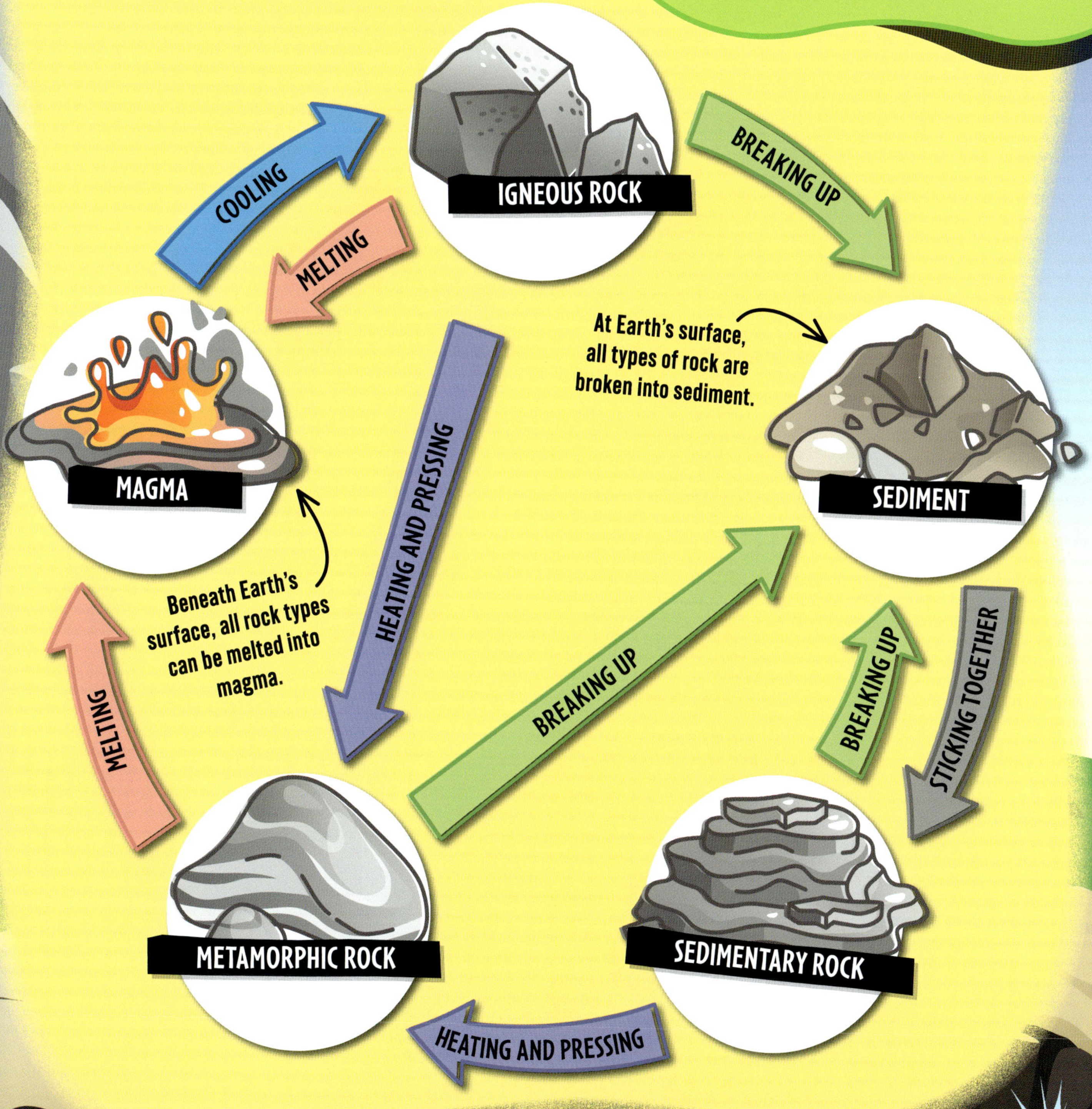

IGNEOUS ROCK

BREAKING UP

COOLING

MELTING

At Earth's surface, all types of rock are broken into sediment.

MAGMA

HEATING AND PRESSING

SEDIMENT

Beneath Earth's surface, all rock types can be melted into magma.

BREAKING UP

BREAKING UP

STICKING TOGETHER

MELTING

METAMORPHIC ROCK

SEDIMENTARY ROCK

HEATING AND PRESSING

HOT INSIDE

Earth's heat causes the rock cycle.

Beneath Earth's cool surface, our planet is superhot. Deep underground is hot rock that is soft enough to flow. This endless movement drives the rock cycle.

Earth's layers

When Earth formed, around 4.5 billion years ago, it was a superhot mix of melted rock and metal. The metal sank to Earth's center, while the planet's surface cooled into solid rock. Today, our planet has layers, each layer hotter than the layer above.

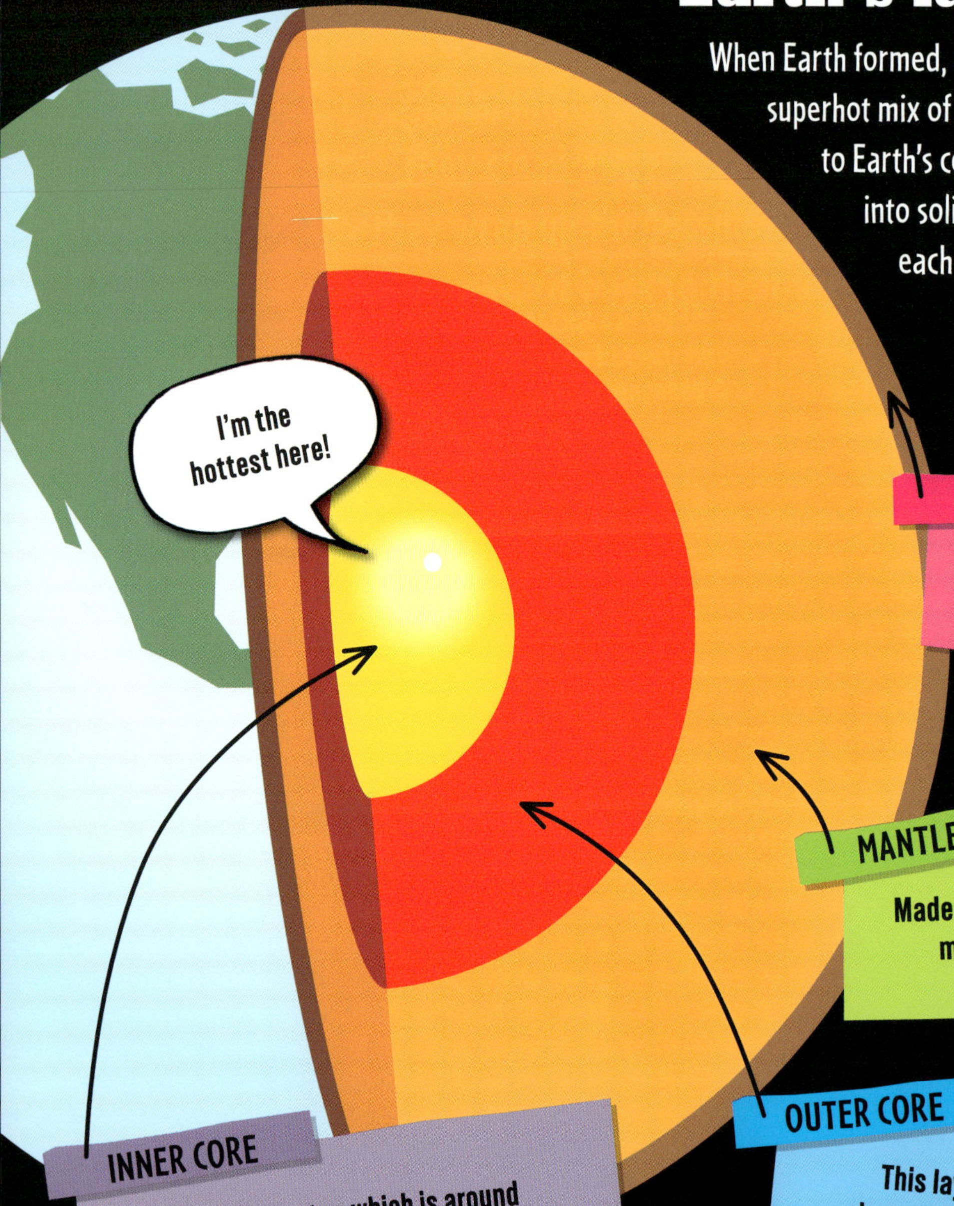

I'm the hottest here!

CRUST

Earth's outer layer is cool, solid rock.

MANTLE

Made of rock that is partly melted, the mantle reaches about 6,700°F (3,700°C).

OUTER CORE

This layer, made of melted iron and nickel, reaches about 9,000°F (5,000°C).

INNER CORE

At Earth's center, which is around 10,800°F (6,000°C), superhot iron and nickel are squeezed into a solid ball.

Cracked crust

Earth's crust (along with the top of the mantle) is made up of 15 to 20 pieces, called tectonic plates. The plates fit together like the pieces of a jigsaw, but they move slowly against each other as they float on the hot, slowly flowing rock below. This movement makes rocks change. The places were plates meet are called boundaries.

DIVERGENT BOUNDARY

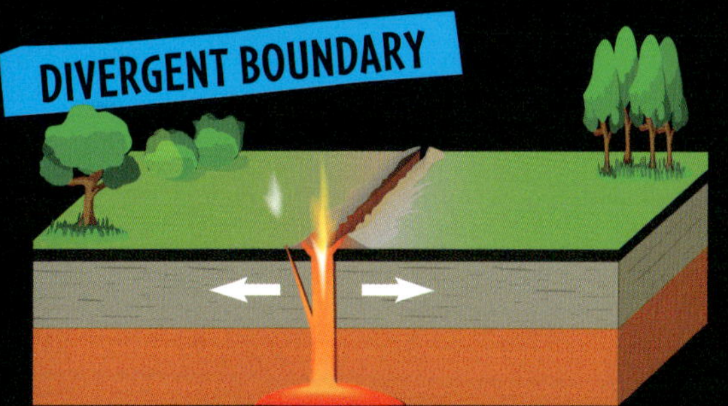

Where plates are moving apart, melted rock surges up from the mantle. It then cools, forming igneous rock.

CONVERGENT BOUNDARY

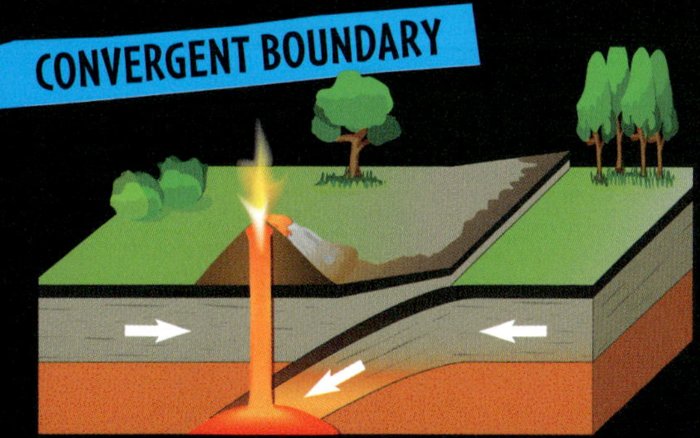

Where plates are moving towards each other, rock is heated and pressed, making metamorphic rock. Surface rock is pushed down into the hot mantle, where it melts and rises to the surface, making igneous rock.

Your turn!

Experiment with tectonic plates!

You will need two plastic-coated playing cards, shaving cream, a tray, and an adult to help.

1. Squirt shaving cream into your tray so it covers the bottom. Imagine the foam is the hot rock of Earth's mantle.

2. Place two playing cards on the foam so they are touching each other along one edge. Pressing down a little, push the cards slowly apart. These are divergent (moving apart) plates. What happens to the foam?

3. Now move the cards towards each other, so one moves under the other. These are convergent (moving together) plates. What happens to the foam?

Did you think playing cards were just for fun?

MOVING WATER

Water also affects the rock cycle!

Earth's water is always on the move. This movement is called the water cycle. Without the water cycle, the rock cycle would be very different! Water breaks rock into sediment, carries sediment away, then drops sediment where it becomes sedimentary rock!

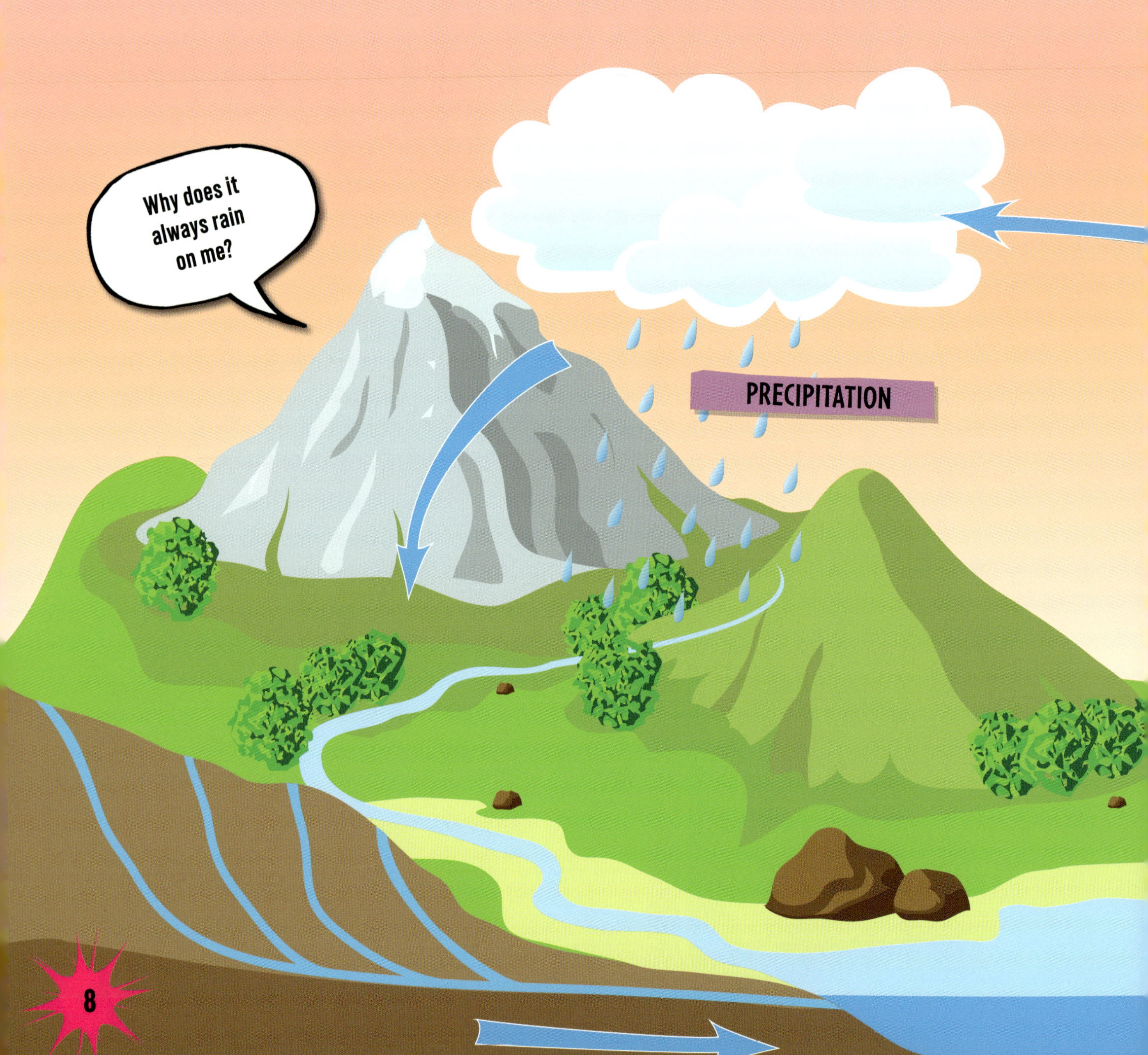

The water cycle

The sun's heat makes water evaporate from oceans and rivers. This means the liquid water turns into a gas, called water vapor. As water vapor rises into the air, it cools. This makes it condense, turning back into a liquid.

Tiny drops of water form clouds. When the drops grow heavy, they fall to the ground as rain—or, if it is very cold, as snow. This is called precipitation. Rain breaks down rock. Rain and snow collect into rivers and streams, which carry along sediment.

It's a fact

More than 120,000 cubic miles (500,000 cu km) of rain or snow fall on Earth each year.

PHOTO QUIZ!

Does this photo show evaporation, condensation, or precipitation? Answer on page 28.

CONSTANT CHANGE

Rocks are changed by powerful processes.

Without the rock cycle, Earth's surface would be flat! But moving tectonic plates and water are constantly changing our planet's rocks. They create processes–from melting to uplift–that give Earth its mountains and valleys.

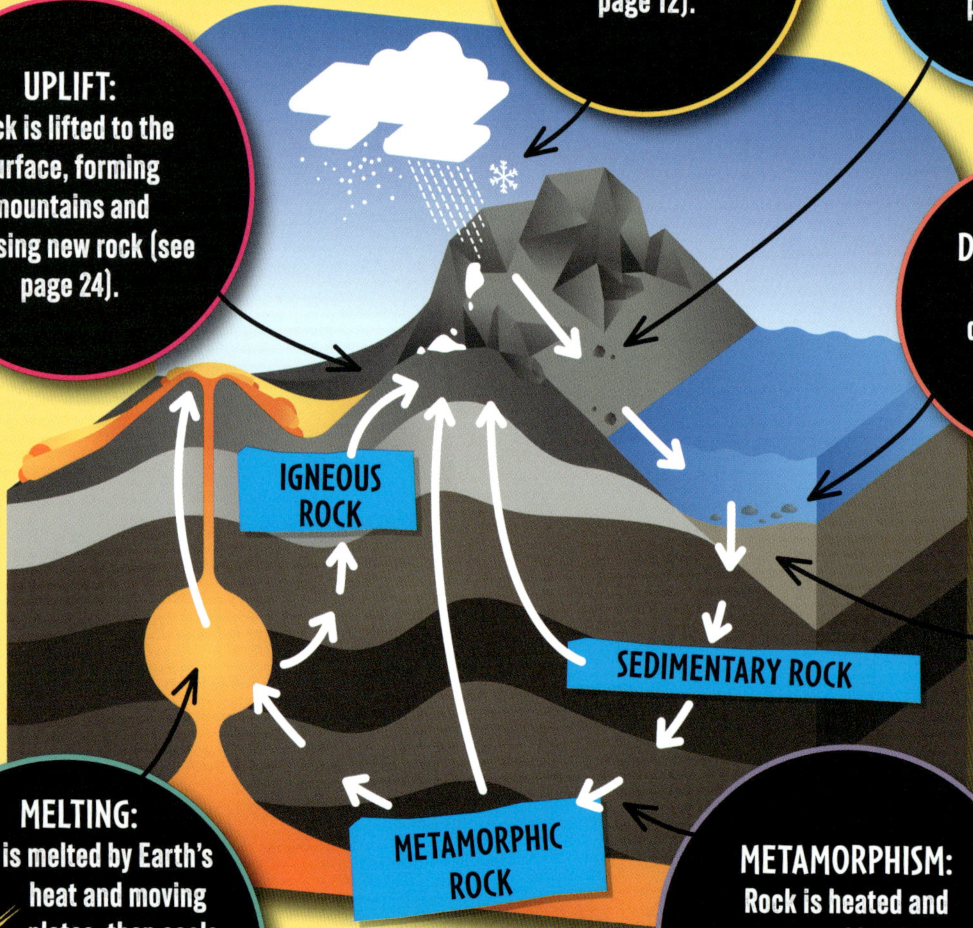

Super seven

Seven key processes play a role in the rock cycle:

Did you know?
It takes from a few thousand years to a few million years for one rock type to change into another rock type.
I am very old indeed.
PHOTO QUIZ!
This building was cut into sandstone cliffs in Petra, Jordan, around 2,000 years ago by the Nabataean people. Sandstone is a rock made from grains of sand that have been pressed together. What type of rock is sandstone: igneous, sedimentary, or metamorphic?
Answer on page 28.

WONDERFUL WEATHERING

Weathering breaks rock into sediment.

Weathering makes rock crumble. A major cause of weathering is the weather, but animals and plants play their part too! Rocks can crumble into sediment tinier than sand or as big as a boulder.

Heat and cold

In hot weather, rocks expand (become larger) a little, but they contract (shrink) again when the temperature falls at night. When this happens day after day, rocks crack and crumble. In addition, rain can soak into rocks, then freeze into ice at night or in winter. Ice takes up more space than water, so it forces the rocks apart.

These granite rocks, known as tors, were weathered by being soaked by rainwater that froze and melted, again and again.

Rainwater and air

Rainwater is slightly acidic, which means it wears away some materials, such as the sedimentary rock limestone. Rainwater weathers deep cracks and caves in limestone. Rocks that contain iron, such as ironstone, are weathered by a mix of rainwater and air. The rocks' surface rusts and crumbles, like an old iron nail.

A "limestone pavement" is made when rainwater weathers cracks in limestone.

Plants and animals

Growing tree roots and burrowing animals can break rock apart. Humans can wear down the rock of walking paths. Some living things, such as algae, release chemicals that break down rock so they can feed on its minerals.

This rock has been weathered by sea animals called piddocks, which grind the rock with their shells to make a safe burrow.

QUICK QUIZ!

Which of these does NOT play a part in weathering: burrowing rabbits, rainwater, or loud singing? Answer on page 28.

It's a fact

The world's longest limestone cave system is Mammoth Cave, in Kentucky, which has more than 420 miles (680 km) of passageways.

CARRIED AWAY

Erosion carries away sediment.

After weathering has broken rock, erosion carries away the pieces. There are four main causes of erosion: water, wind, ice, and gravity. Across the world, erosion is shaping our planet's surface, making valleys and jagged peaks.

Water

Streams and rivers carry sediment in their water. At the coast, waves wear down cliffs and carry away the sediment, leaving caves, arches, and freestanding rocks called stacks.

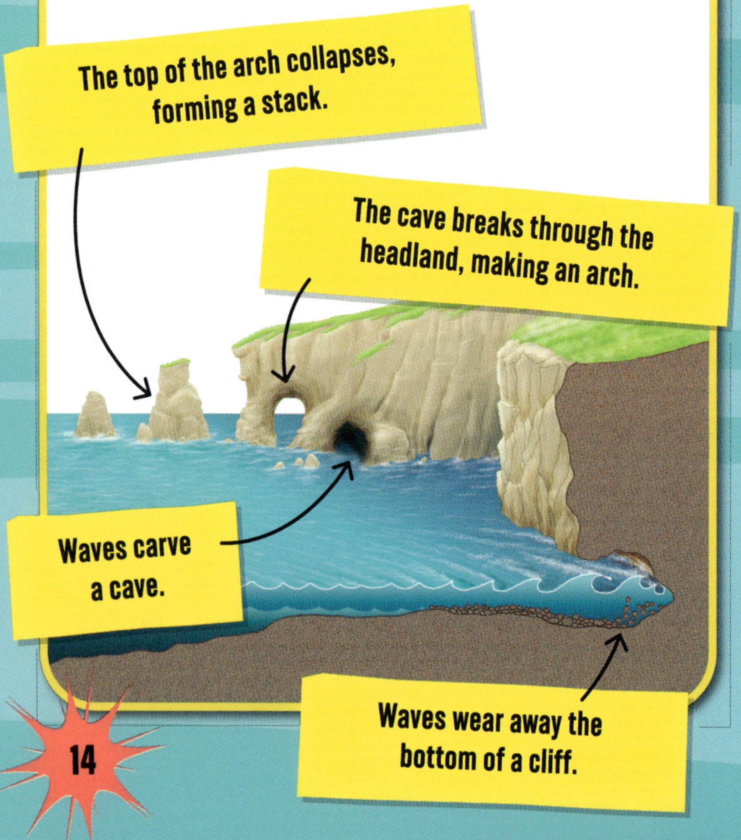

The top of the arch collapses, forming a stack.

The cave breaks through the headland, making an arch.

Waves carve a cave.

Waves wear away the bottom of a cliff.

Wind

The wind hurls sand at rock, wearing it away, and then carries away the sediment. This process can form strange rock formations, such as caves and mushroom rocks.

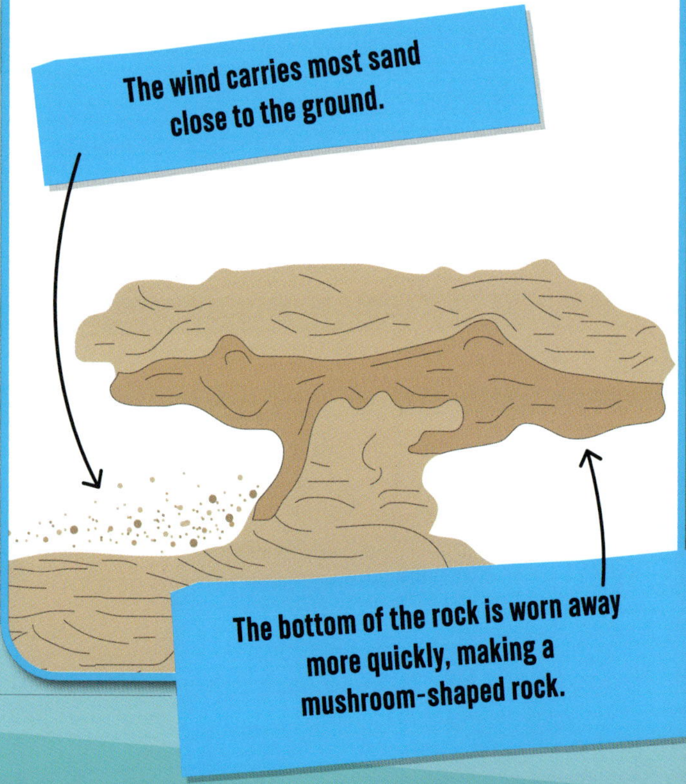

The wind carries most sand close to the ground.

The bottom of the rock is worn away more quickly, making a mushroom-shaped rock.

Ice

On mountaintops, snow packs and freezes together to form great masses of ice called glaciers. As glaciers slide slowly downhill, they pick up rocks from the ground and carry them along, gouging out U-shaped valleys.

A glacier carves a U-shaped valley with a flat floor and steep sides.

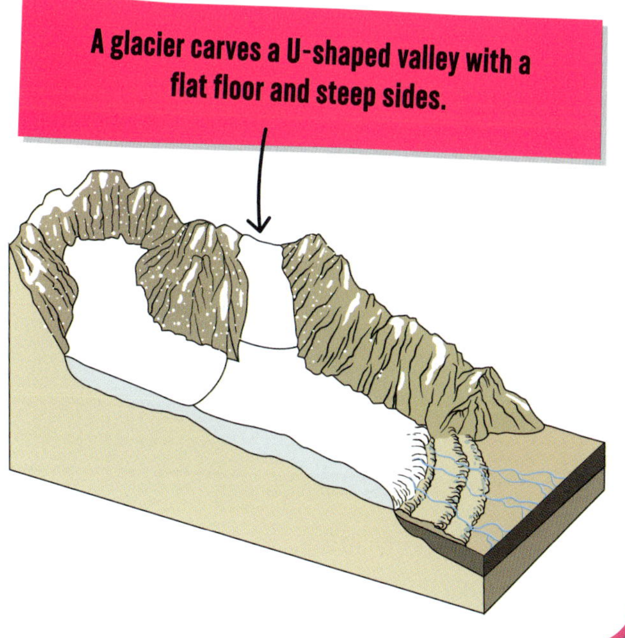

Gravity

Gravity is a force that pulls all objects towards the center of Earth. After rocks on cliffs and mountains have been weathered, gravity makes them fall.

Fallen sediment forms a pile of loose stones called scree.

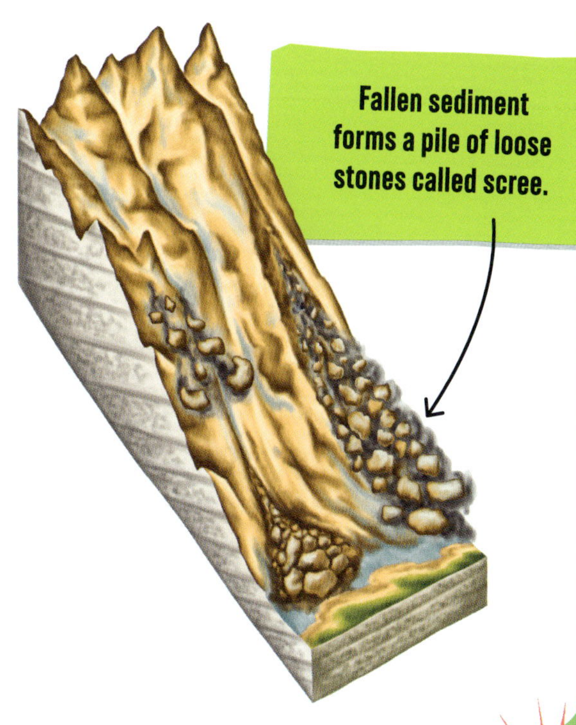

DROP IT!

Deposition drops sediment.

Water, wind, ice, and gravity transport sediment until they run out of energy. Then sediment is dropped. This is deposition. Piles and strips of sediment make amazing landscape features, such as beaches and sandspits.

Shaping with sediment

Sediment is dropped where the movement of water, wind, or ice slows down. Large, heavy pieces of sediment are dropped sooner than light pieces. Gravity drops sediment at the bottom of slopes.

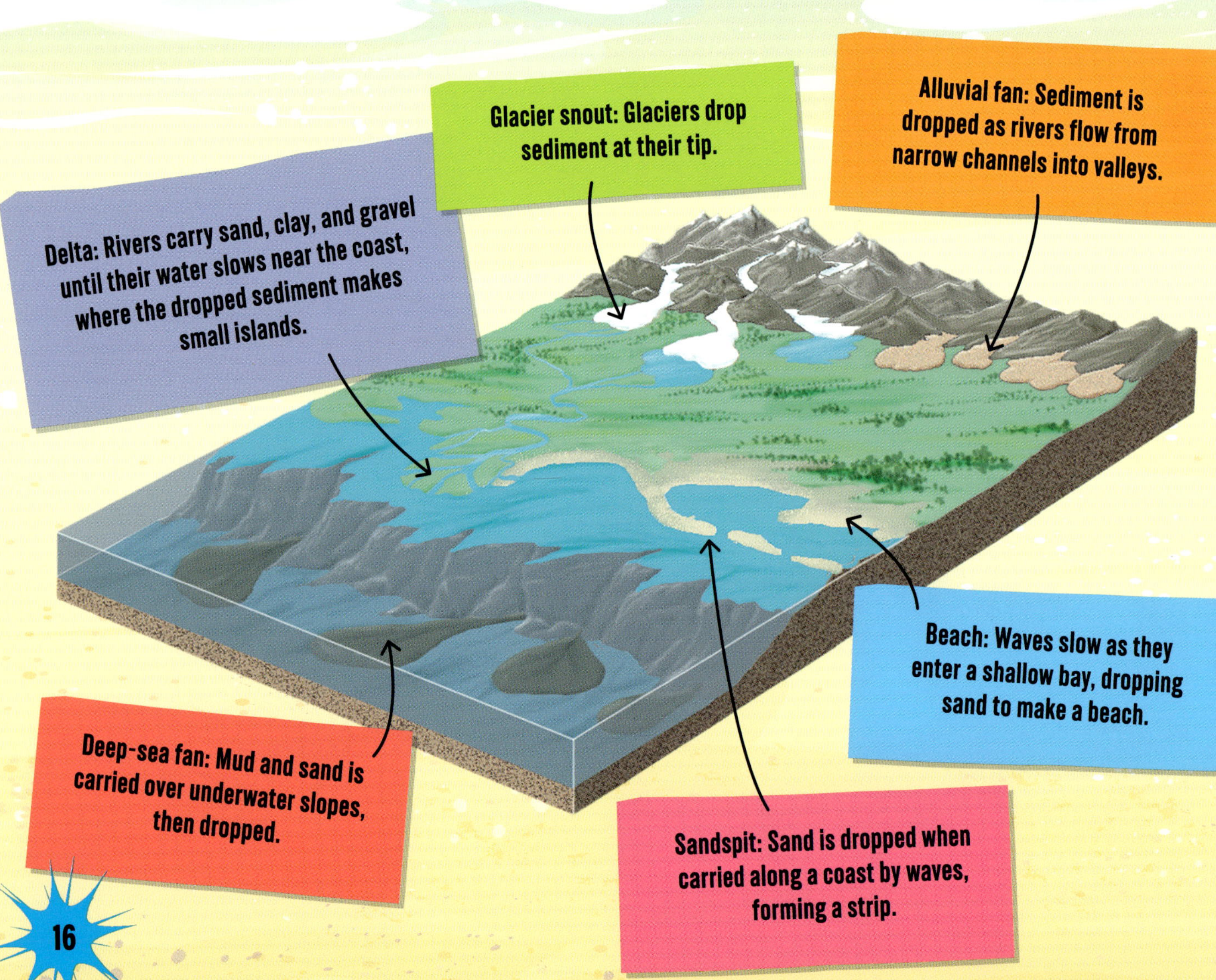

Create your own sediment transport and deposition!

You will need a baking tray, sand, gravel, pitcher of water, and an adult to help you.

1. In half of your baking tray, pile up your sand into a slope. This is your mountain! The bottom of the mountain should run across the middle of the tray. Leave the other half of the tray empty. This area will be your ocean.

2. Make a riverbed in your sand mountain by smoothing an S-shaped dip, running from the top of the mountain to the ocean. Place a few pieces of gravel along your riverbed.

3. Pour a little water into the top of the riverbed and watch the water flow downhill.

4. What happens to the sediment in your riverbed? Is the gravel transported as far as the sand? Where is the sediment deposited?

Baking tray

Sand

Gravel

Pitcher of water

I know I built that sandcastle somewhere around here ...

Did you know?

The longest sandspit is the 70-mile (112 km) Arabat Spit, on Eastern Europe's Crimean Peninsula.

SUPER SEDIMENTARY

Sedimentary rocks are made of sediment.

After sediment has been deposited, it can be buried and pressed until it hardens into rock. Sedimentary rock can also form when the water carrying sediment turns to gas.

Cementation

Deposited sediment builds up in layers. The weight of sediment pushes down on the sediment below, pressing it together. This is called compaction. The water is squeezed out of the sediment. Minerals grow in the spaces between sediment pieces, gluing them together. This is called cementation.

Crystallization

When shallow water is filled with sediment, the water can sometimes evaporate but leave behind the sediment. This happens easily in a shallow pool in a hot, dry place. The sediment sticks slowly together, forming rock. This is called crystallization.

A desert rose is a rock made as water evaporated, leaving behind sand and minerals.

Make your own "sedimentary rock."

You will need paper cups, a spoon, sand, water, sugar, and an adult to help.

1. Put two spoonfuls of sand in a paper cup.

2. In a different cup, mix spoonfuls of water with five spoonfuls of sugar until the sugar dissolves (can no longer be seen).

3. Stir the sugar water into the sand.

4. Leave your "sedimentary rock" to dry, then tear off the paper cup. Now leave the rock to harden for around three days.

5. Examine your rock. Can you see the grains of sugar that have cemented together your sand grains, like the minerals that stick together real sedimentary rock?

MAGICAL METAMORPHIC

Earth's heat and moving plates make metamorphic rock.

Any type of rock can be changed into metamorphic rock. The word "metamorphic" comes from the ancient Greek words for "changing form." When a rock is metamorphosed, its texture and hardness are changed.

Changing rock

For a rock to be changed into metamorphic rock, it must be exposed to great heat, immense pressure, or hot liquid. However, if the rock gets so hot or is squeezed so tightly that it melts, it becomes igneous rock instead (see page 22). There are four main ways in which rock can be metamorphosed.

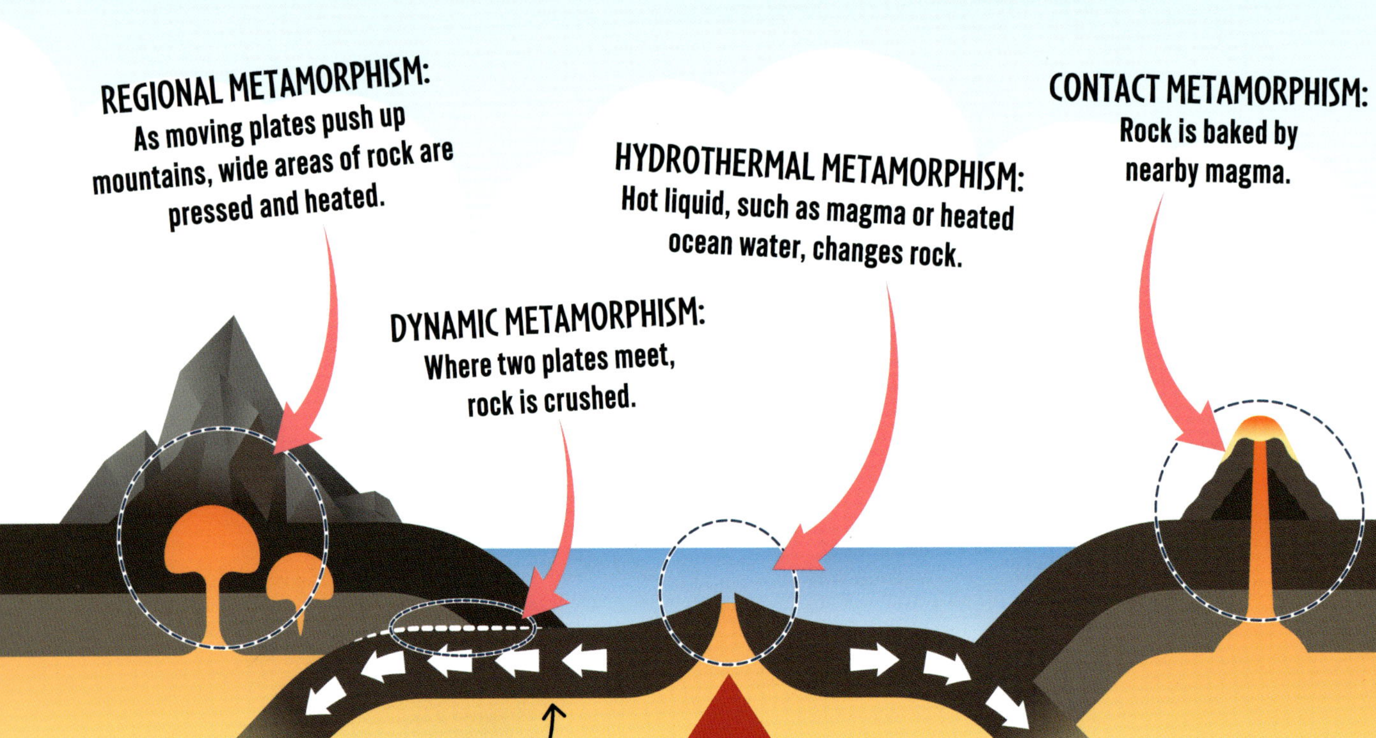

PHOTO QUIZ!

The rocks on the left are sedimentary rocks. The rocks on the right are metamorphic rocks. If each of the three rocks on the left is metamorphosed, which of the three metamorphic rocks does it turn into? Answers on page 28.

INCREDIBLE IGNEOUS

Igneous rock is made when melted rock cools into solid rock.

Igneous rock is made from melted rock, called magma. Magma is found in the heat of the upper mantle and lower crust. Melted rock can cool into igneous rock inside the crust or at Earth's surface.

Inside or outside

When magma surges up through layers of solid rock, it can cool inside the crust. This makes intrusive igneous rock. After magma spills from a volcano, it is known as lava. Lava cools in the air or seawater. This makes extrusive igneous rock.

Growing grains

Inside the crust, intrusive igneous rock cools slowly. This gives its minerals time to grow into large crystals, made as particles of the mineral join together in a repeating pattern. In contrast, extrusive igneous rocks cool quickly, so their crystals are small.

This extrusive igneous rock cooled so quickly its crystals had no time to grow, giving it a glassy texture.

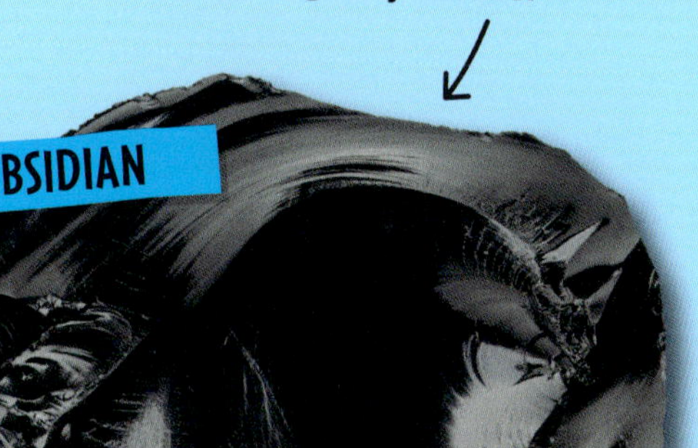

OBSIDIAN

This intrusive igneous rock cooled slowly, giving it large crystals and a rough texture.

GRANITE

I formed slowly, but I got there in the end!

Don't tell anyone, but we weren't actually made by a giant ...

Did you know?

The Giant's Causeway, in Northern Ireland, is made of basalt, an extrusive igneous rock. As the lava cooled, it cracked into regular shapes.

MOVING UP

Uplift lifts rocks to the surface.

The movement of tectonic plates can push rock upwards, forming mountains. Rock is also uplifted when the rock above is worn away, making the lower rock expand upwards. Uplift exposes new rock, which is then weathered and eroded!

Making fold mountains

Fold mountains are made when tectonic plates are moving towards each other. Rocks are folded upwards, a little like a crumpled piece of paper.

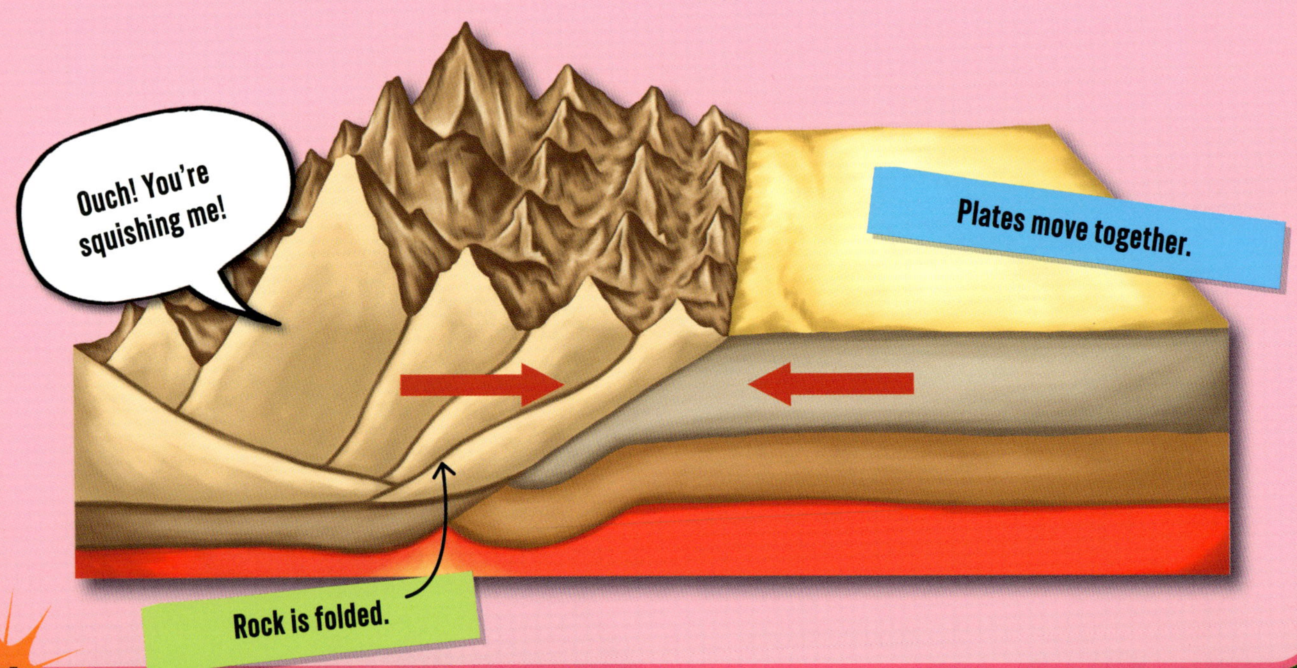

Making fault-block mountains

These mountains are made when the crust is cracked by plate movements. Some blocks are uplifted while others are forced downwards.

There are fossils of ancient sea creatures in the limestone of Mount Everest, which is the world's highest mountain at 29,032 feet (8,849 m) tall.

PHOTO QUIZ!

Can you name this famous Asian mountain range, home to Mount Everest? The range formed due to folding as the Indo-Australian Plate and Eurasian Plate collided. Answer on page 28.

LOOK OUT!

Look for evidence of the rock cycle!

When you go for a walk, search for signs of the rock cycle. If you live in a city, where there is little exposed rock, look out for old stone buildings with weathered bricks and steps worn away by countless feet!

Watch for weathering

Weathered rocks are cracked, crumbling, or shedding their outer layers.

Discover deposition

Rivers deposit sediment on the insides of their bends, where the water's flow is slowest.

Look for layers

Layers are found where different sediments were deposited on each other over thousands of years. In addition, sedimentary rocks may form on top of igneous or metamorphic rocks—and then be covered by cooled lava!

Find folds

Rocks are folded by the pushing and squeezing of moving plates.

PHOTO QUIZ!

Examine this photo of the Grand Canyon, which was eroded by the Colorado River. Which of the exposed layers of rock are 1.8 billion years old and which are around 270 million years old? Answer on page 28.

QUICK QUIZ ANSWERS

PAGE 5

Earth's youngest rocks are less than 1 year old, as they are made of melted rock that has recently erupted from a volcano.

PAGE 9

Rain is a type of precipitation.

PAGE 11

Sandstone is a sedimentary rock made from grains of sand that have been cemented together.

PAGE 13

Loud singing cannot weather rock.

PAGE 15

Waves eroded the stack and arches.

PAGE 21

Limestone becomes marble, mudstone becomes slate and sandstone becomes quartzite.

PAGE 25

The mountain range is called the Himalayas. It stretches across parts of Bhutan, China, India, Nepal, and Pakistan.

PAGE 27

The layers at the bottom of the canyon are 1.8 billion years old while those at the top are around 270 million years old.

NOW TEST YOUR KNOWLEDGE!

1 **Which group of rocks are made from magma or lava that has cooled?**

a) Sedimentary

b) Igneous

c) Metamorphic

2 **What is sandstone made from?**

a) Sand

b) Lava

c) Super-heated granite

3 **What makes a desert rose?**

a) Desert rose seeds

b) Evaporation from shallow pools

c) Weathering by piddocks

4 **The Giant's Causeway was made by which process?**

a) Hardworking giants

b) Wave erosion

c) Lava cooling and cracking

5 **Limestone is weathered by which liquid?**

a) Lava

b) Rainwater

c) Sugar water

6 **What can make folds in rocks?**

a) Moving tectonic plates

b) Precipitation

c) Deposition

ANSWERS ON PAGE 31

GLOSSARY

burrow – to dig a hole or tunnel

cementation – the sticking together of sediment

core – Earth's innermost layer, made of superhot metal

crust – Earth's outer layer, made of solid rock

delta – an area of low land where a river divides into smaller streams before entering the ocean

deposition – the laying down of sediment carried by water, wind, ice, or gravity

erosion – the movement of rock from one place to another

evaporation – when a liquid turns into a gas

fossil – the remains of an ancient animal or plant

glacier – a slowly moving mass of ice formed on a cold mountaintop or near the poles

igneous rock – a rock formed when melted rock cools and hardens

lava – melted rock that is above Earth's surface

magma – melted rock that is beneath Earth's surface

mantle – the layer of Earth between the core and the crust, made of rock that is partly melted

metamorphic rock – a rock formed when any type of rock is changed by great heat or pressure

mineral – a solid that forms naturally in the ground or in water

precipitation – rain, snow, or hail, which fall from clouds

rock – a solid mix of different minerals

rock cycle – a series of processes that create and change the rocks in Earth's crust

rust – a flaky, red-brown coating that forms on the surface of iron

sand – grains of rock, coral, or shell

sediment – fragments of rock, mineral, dead animals, or dead plants

sedimentary rock – a rock formed from hardened sediment

tectonic plate – one of the massive slabs of rock that form Earth's crust and upper mantle

uplift – the slow lifting of the rocks in Earth's crust

volcano – a hole in Earth's crust though which hot, liquid rock can escape

weathering – the breaking down of rock

FURTHER READING

BOOKS

Brink, Tracy Vander. *Igneous Rocks.* New York, NY: Seahorse Publishing, 2023.

McDougal, Anna. *The Rock Cycle.* Buffalo, NY: Enslow Publishing, 2023.

Rogers, Marie. *Exploring the Rock Cycle.* New York, NY: PowerKids Press, 2021.

WEBSITES

www.dkfindout.com/us/earth/rock-cycle/
Explore the rock cycle and other Earth science information at this website for kids.

https://education.nationalgeographic.org/resource/resource-library-rock-cycle/
Check out lots of articles that have to do with rocks and the rock cycle here.

Answers: 1b, 2a, 3b, 4c, 5b, 6a

INDEX